IT'S THE GOSPEL TRUTH

IT'S THE GOSPEL TRUTH

HUMOROUS MEMORIES FROM THE PREACHER'S WIFE

ANNEAL TRIPLETT LEDBETTER

Edited by Hannah Ledbetter Powell

Text contributor: James Ervin Ledbetter, Jr., Ph.D.

Cover and photograph design: Janet Ledbetter Nummi

Front cover illustration: Evelyn Guire Allen

Back cover portrait: Judy Greene Prevost

DEDICATION

For Arbie Runion,
dear friend, faithful companion, compassionate caregiver
and guardian of the manuscript.

TABLE OF CONTENTS

DEDICATION...v

PREFACE ix

1 WOMEN IN THE CHURCH 1

2 WISDOM WITH AGE...5

3 BLESSED ARE THE CHILDREN 7

4 LET US PRAY...11

5 PREPARING FOR THE MINISTRY.........................13

6 MINISTERING TO THE FLOCK 15

7 ANNOUNCEMENTS 19

8 PREACHING THE GOSPEL.....................................21

9 SPECIAL OCCASIONS..25

ABOUT THE AUTHOR...29

ACKNOWLEDGEMENTS...37

PREFACE

By her Children, James Ervin Ledbetter, Jr. and Hannah Ledbetter Powell
"A merry heart doeth good like a medicine."(Proverbs 17:22)

Our mother Anneal Triplett Ledbetter was born and raised in Lenoir, North Carolina. She was baptized, married and even provided detailed instructions for her Celebration of Life at the First Baptist Church where her parents were charter members.

She met our father James Ervin Ledbetter, a Tennessee resident who came from five generations of Baptist ministers, while they were both students at Southern Baptist Theological Seminary in Louisville, Kentucky. He was "practice preaching" or what was known as "street preaching" in downtown Louisville and she was handing out religious tracts when they first met and the common bond was established through their dedication to religious work. As the story goes when her father, a successful businessman, learned that she wanted to marry a minister, his response was, "He won't be able to keep you in shoes!" Although her father refused to give her away, a "higher calling" prevailed and they walked down the aisle together in marriage on September 12, 1940, and spent their fifty-two years of married life in the ministry.

Mother was a very strong, loving and unique woman. Although born in 1917, she loved studying and teaching the Bible and was never hindered by social convention. She received her Master's Degree in Religious Education and became a well-known speaker, humorist, counselor and teacher in her community. She loved to make people laugh! She was also known for her compassion and spent many hours helping others with their personal and religious struggles. She was a wonderful mother and instilled a strong love of God and family and kindness to others in both of our lives. One of the greatest lessons we learned from her was to enjoy life to its fullest. She often quoted

Philippians 4:11, "for I have learned, in whatsoever state I am, therewith to be content."

During her ninety-eight years of Christian service, she collected many true stories which she compiled into handwritten notes entitled, "It's The Gospel Truth". She often said that her stories could not be published until some of the people mentioned had "gone on to glory." Our mother passed away in 2015, so in tribute we feel the time has finally come to publish her stories. Some of the names have been changed to protect the innocent, but if you happen to recognize a friend, relative or yourself, please know that she loved you all and would never wish you any hurt or embarrassment.

Her Sunday School Class at the First Baptist Church in Lenoir North Carolina that began as the "Young Marrieds Class" evolved into a long-term mission that she honored for over twenty-five years as those in her class never seemed to "graduate". They became her second family of loving friends, several of whom were at her bedside when she passed away. One person who remained by her side as her health declined was Arbie Runion, to whom this book is dedicated. Arbie was such a loving friend and loyal caretaker throughout Mother's final years. Mother's pastor, Dr. David Smith, noted at her funeral that he thought they could sometimes read each other's thoughts and that certainly rang true. As Arbie now struggles with her own health issues, we want to ensure that she receives this book as both a gift and a heartfelt thank-you for the love and care that she provided for our mother.

1 WOMEN IN THE CHURCH

"Who can find a virtuous woman? For her price is far above rubies."
(Proverbs 31:10)

While living in LaFollette, Tennessee, a church in the mountains needed a speaker for a special occasion. They tried to get several different men and were unable to find anyone available. Finally they asked the associational missionary to send someone and he asked me to go. I knew they didn't want anyone from the First Baptist Church and they certainly didn't want a woman, but I agreed to go. When I got there, I could feel a very real disappointment as the preacher got up to introduce me. He said, "This here is Sister Ledbetter. We could have done with a poorer speaker but we couldn't find one." After I spoke the preacher said, "Sister Ledbetter, you come back any time you want to. You are just as common as you can be!"

I was speaking at a church in the county and the preacher prayed for me. He said, "Lord we thank you for Mrs. Ledbetter. We thank you for her physical and spiritual assets." When we got home my husband said he thought my physical assets were getting a little out of hand!

At another speaking engagement, the preacher introduced me by saying, "I really don't need to introduce our speaker, she's too well known already."

We got married on September 12, 1940 on Thursday. We went to Ervin's church in Bristol, Tennessee on Sunday. I looked around for someone with a kind face to sit by and noticed a friendly looking older man and woman. After the service the man stuck out his hand to shake mine and said, "Sister Ledbetter,

Praise God you can't sing." I didn't know I couldn't! Later I found out that the former preacher's wife had considered herself an accomplished vocalist and had apparently worn out her talent.

In the old days women didn't wear slacks or shorts and when they finally began to wear them, many people were shocked and dismayed. I heard a local preacher on the radio that was preaching against women wearing shorts and he said, "As I came to church this morning, I saw a woman that had on shorts so short she almost didn't have on anything at all! Praise God! Hallelujah!"

In Lenoir City, Tennessee my husband I went to visit a lady that hadn't been to church in a while. When she came to the door she had on a pair of slacks. When she saw who was at the door, her mouth gaped open and she cried out, "Preacher if I'd known you were coming, I wouldn't have had my pants on!"

Also in Lenoir City when women first started wearing shorts to town some of the preachers decided they would go before the city council and get an ordinance passed that women shouldn't come to town unless properly attired. When the matter was presented to the council, Brother Blackman said, "Well I'm sixty years old and I'm too old for it to bother me, but if it bothers the preachers, I move we do something about it." That was the end of that!

One Sunday the preacher was preaching about gossip and he said, "I just can't stand women running around with dirty tales!"

One preacher was trying to expound on the seriousness of the sin of some women. In his effort to declare its gravity he said, "I'll tell you folks, if I had a wife like that I'd just get me another one!"

One hot summer day the preacher met a woman on the street and they both commented on the weather. She said, "It's so hot, I'm going to go home and take off my clothes and see if I can't get cooled off." The preacher not thinking said, "I believe I'll just go home with you and do the same thing."

A guest preacher was staying in a hotel during an out of town revival. On the last day his wife was coming to attend the service and they were invited to stay in one of the member's home. When the preacher went to check out he said to the desk clerk, "I have enjoyed staying here so much but tonight I'm going to spend the night with one of the good ladies from the church."

In the old days there was a woman that always rode sidesaddle to church on her horse. One Sunday the horse reared up and her skirt flew up. The preacher had on a big hat and he grabbed it off and held it in front of her as he called out, "More hats or more help!"

Once we were having a revival and after the morning service, we were having lunch in the Fellowship Hall. The women preparing the meal took the guest speaker aside and told him that when he smelled the bread cooking, he should wrap up his sermon because lunch would be ready. The evangelist was preaching away and the odor of bread baking filled the sanctuary. The evangelist said, "Well I smell the women in the basement so I'd better end my sermon".

In one of the churches we served, the women and children sat on one side and the men sat on the other. One Sunday, the Baptist Young People's Union Director was trying to get people to return that evening for BYPU. He looked at the men and said, "You adults some back to the service tonight". Then he quickly looked over at the women and said, "You adulteresses come too!'

A preacher said to his wife, "You don't deserve a husband like me!" Her answer, "I don't deserve sinus trouble either, but I've got it!"

A revival preacher explained that he didn't like to eat dinner until after the service, so one woman prepared to serve the meal after church. When he got there she said to him, "Preacher you might as well have 'et' first!"

2 WISDOM WITH AGE

"Happy is the man that findeth wisdom, and the man that getteth understanding." (Proverbs 3:13)

A Texas church had a new pastor and someone asked one of the deacons if his new preacher was a good speaker. The man said, "He is just like a Texas longhorn bull. He usually has two good points and a lot of bull in between."

An older man was driving down a one way street. A policeman stopped him and asked, "Where do you think you're going?" The man answered, "I don't know, but I must be late – everyone is coming back!"

The preacher asked one elderly gentleman, "Are you going to Heaven?" He replied, "Well, I reckon I will if I keep my health and live long enough,"

In Crossville, Tennessee, there was an older man that pulled out into the road in his car and bumped into the preacher's car. The police came to assess the damage and the policeman asked, "Did you have your blinkers on?" The man replied, "I guess I did. I put on everything the old lady laid out this morning."

I overheard a young man whisper to one of the more mature ladies in the church, "Ma'am, you're stockings are twisted." She answered, "You're wrong young man; I'm not wearing any stockings."

Our family doctor told the story of an eighty- year-old parishioner who came to him for a physical exam prior to marrying a twenty-five- year-old girl. The doctor told him that the physical exertion could be fatal and the man replied, "Well, so be it. If she dies, she dies!"

One older bachelor wanted a wife and he finally met a woman he thought might be suitable. He prayed for God's guidance on whether they should marry. When Christmas came he gave her bookends and she gave him two books. He took that as a sure sign that they should marry.

One elderly man said to his girlfriend, "I'm getting a little forgetful. Did I ask you to marry me last night?" His girlfriend replied, "Well someone did, but I've forgotten who it was."

One of my favorite exercises for Senior Citizen Groups was to have them take a test. You are getting old if:

- All the names in your date book end with M.D.
- You decide to procrastinate and never get around to it.
- You look forward to a dull evening.
- You walk with your head held high trying to get used to your bifocals.
- Your knees buckle, but you belt won't.
- Dialing long distance wears you out.
- You burn the midnight oil after 9:00 p.m.
- Your back goes out more than you do.
- You sink your teeth into a steak and they stay there.
- Your broad mind has changed places with your narrow waist.

3 BLESSED ARE THE CHILDREN

"Suffer little children, and forbid them not, to come unto me: for of such is the kingdom of heaven." (Matthew 19:14)

A Sunday School teacher asked the children, "Where does God live?" One little boy answered, "I know. He lives in our bathroom." The teacher asked, "How do you know?" He said, "My dad yells at the bathroom door every morning, 'Good Lord, are you still in there'?"

A Sunday School teacher of young boys and girls asked, "Why do people call me a Christian?" One child responded, "Because they don't know you?"

A Vacation Bible School teacher pointed to the flag and asked, "Do any of you know what this is?" "Yes, I know" replied a little girl named Amy. "It's the flag of our country." The teacher said, "Good, now tell me the name of our country." Amy replied, "Tis of Thee".

The preacher told a little girl, "You have your shoes on the wrong feet." The little girl answered, "Well these are the only feet I have!'

A little boy said to his mother, "When I grow up I want to be a preacher. Will that be okay?" She answered, "I guess so, but why do you want to be a preacher?" He replied, "Well, I've got to go to church anyway and since I hate to sit still, I'd rather go to church and stand up and holler like the preacher does."

A woman whose husband didn't come to church asked the preacher to come for a meal hoping he could influence her husband to begin attending services with them. While they waited for her to get the food on the table, their little boy kept looking at the preacher. Finally he said, "Daddy look at the preacher. His head ain't so flat!"

At another home the little girl asker her mother, "Isn't that roast pork we're having for dinner?" Her mother replied, "Yes it is. Why do you ask?" The little girl looked at the preacher who was having dinner with them and said, "Well Daddy is so silly. He said we were having an old mutton head for dinner."

Six-year-old Jimmy complained that he had a stomach ache. His mother said, "Your stomach probably hurts because it's empty. You'll feel better if you have something in it." The preacher stopped by to visit them that evening and while he was there, he mentioned that he had a headache. Jimmy said, "It hurts because it's empty. It would feel better if you had something in it."

A janitor in our church and his wife had a new baby. When he came to church the next day, the preacher congratulated him and asked, "What did you name the new baby?" "Onix" the man replied. The preacher said, "Well that's very unusual. How did you choose that name?" The man answered, "Because this one was so *onixpected*".

A preacher visited a home where triplets had been born. The preacher said, "I understand the stork has smiled upon you Brother Jones." Mr. Jones replied, "No preacher, he plumb laughed out loud!"

The preacher was visiting in a home and as he was leaving, he asked if could have a prayer with the family. Their little boy blurted out, "With our clothes on? It's not even bedtime!"

One preacher asked a young boy what he liked best about the sermon. The boy answered, "It was short."

The preacher said to his congregation, "The people in this church are so thoughtful. They are dedicating a plaque to all of those who died in the service." A little boy asked loudly, "Did they die in the morning or evening service?"

Once Sunday while Ervin was preaching, a little boy cried out, "Just take me out and whip me!"

The polio epidemic was spreading throughout the United States in the late 1940's. Our son James had just learned to walk and we were so proud. I got him dressed one morning and when he stood up, he was having great difficulty walking. I was terrified! We were living in Lenoir City, Tennessee, at that time and we rushed him to the pediatrician in Knoxville. The doctor examined him thoroughly. He then picked up James' shoes for inspection. He reached down into the toe of one shoe and pulled out his rolled up socks from the day before!

4 LET US PRAY

"And all things, whatsoever ye shall ask in prayer, believing, ye shall receive." (Matthew 21:22)

At a church in Caldwell County my husband was holding a revival. Preacher Davis was the pastor there and he called upon one of the deacons to pray before he preached. The good brother began to pray and said, "Oh Lord, bless our dear pastor, take care of him and protect him. We know the old devil is at work all the time!"

In one country church an old man would sit by the window in the summer and spit tobacco out the window. Sometimes he wasn't such a good shot and would leave a mess. My husband thought he would "cure" him so he told me he was going to call on him to pray sometime when his mouth was full. One night the timing was just right and Ervin said, "Brother John will you pray for us?" John replied, "I don't feel led" and continued to chew.

One older brother would get louder and louder when he prayed. One morning the man sitting next to him pulled on his coat and said, "The Lord is not deaf". The man replied, "He ain't nervous either" and continued to pray loudly.

Preacher John was praying for a wife. He met a woman named Grace but he had trouble discerning the will of God concerning love and whether she was the right woman. On Sunday he came in late to church and the congregation was singing, "He will give us Grace and Glory". John exclaimed, "Well, Praise God" and he married her.

A lady got a call to come to the school because her son was sick. When she got there, the school nurse suggested she take him on to the doctor. When she got to the doctor's office, she had to wait and wait. He finally gave her a prescription and when she got to the drug store, it was closed and she had to hunt another one. She got the medicine and came back out and she had locked her car keys inside the car. She went back into the store to get a coat hanger to try to get her keys out. She worked and worked and couldn't get them out. About that time a rather seedy-looking young man came up and asked if she needed help. He took the coat hanger from her and within a few minutes had the door open and her keys out. The lady said to the young man, "Thank you – you are such a sweet boy. You must be a Christian!" The man replied, "No ma'am, I ain't no Christian – I just got out of jail this morning." The woman started praising the Lord saying, "Lord I thank you for sending a pro!"

In our church in Crossville, Tennessee, we had a member named Ted Crow. One Sunday the preacher called upon him to pray and he said, "Brother Pray will you crow for us?"

A traffic cop stopped a car and said to the driver, "Did you know you left your wife back there in front of the church?" The man said, "Praise the Lord! I thought I was going deaf!"

One night a man who had been drinking landed in jail. He called the preacher to come get him out. He said, "Preacher I want you to pray the Lord will come and get me out of this place and tell him not to send His son. This is no place for a boy!"

One preacher was on the radio and was praying when his time ran out. The announcer finally said, "Preacher you can stop praying, you've been off the air for over five minutes."

A preacher was praying and he intended to say, "Dear Lord fill these people with zeal and vigor for the Lord's work." Instead he said, "Lord fill these people with veal and ziggor."

One night at a banquet the man in charge realized he had failed to ask anyone to bring the invocation so he got up and asked, "Is there a minister in the dining room?" There was no response so he said, "Well let's thank the Lord!"

5 PREPARING FOR THE MINISTRY

"Study to show thyself approved unto God, a workman that needeth not to be ashamed, rightly dividing the word of truth." (2 Timothy 2:15)

Young preachers have much to learn. One of the most common temptations is to talk too fast and that can sometimes bring much grief. One preacher in his message was using John Bunyan's "Pilgrim's Progress" as an example. In his haste he said, "If you will just look at Pilgrim's Bunions you will see what I mean."

After a young preacher spoke one of the older men said to him, "Our people here are very sympathetic. They know you can't expect much from a preacher when he is in a hurry to get started out."

One young preacher raced through his sermon and one of the good sisters felt she needed to give him a word of encouragement following the service. She said, "Young man, the devil may tempt you to be an auctioneer but you just slow down and serve the Lord!"

A young preacher is always uncertain about how the message was received. One beginner went to one of the older members and asked, "How did I get along today?" The old man replied, "Well Preacher, it seemed to me with all them folks sitting up front with their mouths open listening to you talk, by the time it got back to me there just wasn't much left."

At Mars Hill there was a student that felt called to preach. He had grown up in the mountains with little Bible training. He was reading the scripture in church and came upon Psalm, Roman Numeral 104 and he called it "Pisalem Civ".

Rev. Gordon Greenwell was in the seminary at the same time we were. We often rode together from Louisville to our churches in Tennessee. Gordon always wore his only suit and kept a change of socks in his pocket. Before service he would put on the clean socks and put the ones he had worn in his pocket to take back to school. That Sunday he was preaching and got warm. He intended to pull out his handkerchief to wipe his brow. He later told us that the minute it hit his nose, he knew it was his sock but he kept right on preaching.

One older brother told the young preacher that his sermon was like the peace and mercy of God. The preacher modestly asked, "How was that?" The man replied, "It was like the peace of God because it passeth all understanding and the mercy of God that it lasteth forever."

A young preacher asked a girl to marry him and she refused saying that she wasn't sure she wanted to be married to a preacher. He persuaded her to attend a service on Sunday where he was preaching. After she heard him speak she told him she had changed her mind. She told him he wasn't enough of a preacher to make any difference!

My husband Ervin enjoyed mentoring young ministers. He was especially fond of a young man from Lenoir named Tommy Greene and tried to encourage him as much as possible. Following one of his first sermons, Tommy hurried proudly to Ervin to ask how he'd done. Ervin just shook his hand and said, "Just keep sharpening the axe."

6 MINISTERING TO THE FLOCK

"For even the Son of man came not to be ministered unto,
but to minister." (Mark 1:13)

We were often invited out to eat and one lady asked us to her home. She had the cutest little boy and she had told him to be quiet while the preacher was there. We went to the table and she had prepared some fishcakes in a cornbread stick pan. The little boy took one and quickly took a bite. In a minute he raised his hand to be recognized but his mother shook her head. He yelled out, "But I have to tell you something! There's something dead in this bread!"

My husband Ervin was afraid of getting food that might not be healthy. Refrigeration had not come to some of rural East Tennessee at that time; in fact, not all homes had electricity. He advised me that the gravy was usually hot so to spread it around on everything to kill any germs. We went to a home to eat that Sunday after church and he reminded me again about the gravy. When we got to the table, the cat was up on the table already eating out of the gravy bowl. The woman picked the cat up and said, "Tom, you ought not to have done that!" We went right on with the meal – gravy and all!

Ervin was really afraid of drinking spoiled milk so when he was out of town holding a revival he sent word out that he liked tea to drink. We went to a woman's home for dinner and apparently she had never prepared tea before. She must have boiled it all day and it was as thick as syrup. Every time he drank some of it, she would pour more into his glass and say, "Preacher I fixed this special for you!" He had so much caffeine he wasn't able to sleep for several days!

Another time we were in a home eating and it came time for the pie and Ervin had let his fork go with his plate. He asked the lady if he might have another fork. She took the serving fork out of the chicken, licked it and handed it to him.

People often try to hide things when the preacher visits. One woman came to the door with a cigarette in her hand. When she saw it was the preacher, she closed her hand around the cigarette thinking it would go out, but it didn't. The smoke kept rising out between her fingers and tears came to her eyes but she never acknowledged it. On the next Sunday we noticed that she came to church with a large bandage on her hand.

We visited in another home one day where they had been playing cards. When they saw the preacher had arrived there, they quickly hid the cards under the cushions in a chair. My husband sat down in that chair. As he moved around the cards kept falling out on the floor. By the time we left it looked like the whole deck had fallen out.

A preacher was visiting in a home and they were in the habit of having a small drink with their meal. The preacher asked for milk to drink and the boys at the home slipped a little whiskey in his milk. After the preacher had finished he lifted his eyes toward heaven and said, "Oh Lord what a cow!"

There was a woman in the church who was having emotional problems and her husband brought her to talk to the preacher. After a long session, the preacher said to the man, "I'll show you what she needs" and he hugged her and kissed her on the cheek and said, "She needs this every day." The husband replied, "Well I just don't know if I have time to bring her here every day!"

Once the preacher visited in a home where the husband and wife had a fight. Things were rather tense. The preacher asked the woman, "Did you get hurt in the fracas?" and she replied, "No, but I did get a hard lick on my head!"

A couple came to the preacher for counseling. The preacher pulled the husband aside and said, "I'm so sorry to have to tell you this, but I'm afraid wife's mind is gone." "I'm not surprised" the man replied. "She's been giving me a piece of it every day since we've been married."

Another man brought his wife to the preacher and asked him to tell him what was wrong with her; she just wasn't acting right. The preacher said, "I hate to tell you this but I think she has lost her mind." The man answered, "I don't know how that could be. She hasn't been off the place in years!"

Mrs. Bunning complained so bitterly about her aches and pains that her husband took her to the doctor. The doctor stuck a thermometer in her mouth and said, "Keep quiet for about five minutes." Mrs. Bunning obeyed and was very still. Following the exam, her husband took the doctor aside and asked, "Doctor how much will you take for that thing? That's the quietest she's been in years!"

Preacher Benfield was holding a revival in a church and was staying in a home of one of the members. They had him sleep in an attic room and he couldn't go to sleep because it was so hot. He tried to open a window and it wouldn't open so he decided to just break a window pane and buy them a replacement. He slept like a log that night. The next morning he was surprised to see he had broken the glass out in a bookcase.

A burglar broke into a poor minister's house during the night. When the preacher woke up the man was going through his pants pockets. He told the preacher, "If you stir you are a dead man. I'm hunting for money." The preacher replied, "Let me turn on the light and I'll help you hunt."

The preacher asked a man, "Why don't you go to church?" "Well Preacher, the first time I was ever in a church they threw water on my head. The next time I was in church they hooked me up with a woman for life." The preacher replied, "Well I guess the next time you come will be for your funeral and we will throw dirt on you!"

One man told the preacher, "I'm not interested in coming to church. There are too many hypocrites there." The preacher responded, "But there is always room for one more."

A skeptic asked, "Preacher do you really believe that Jonah was swallowed by a whale?" The preacher said, "I believe the Bible and when I get to heaven I will ask Jonah". The man said, "Well what if Jonah isn't there?" The preacher replied, "Then YOU can ask him."

A minister was out visiting and stopped by the house of one of his members. He knocked on the door and the lady of the house called out, "Is that you angel?" "No" the preacher replied, "but I'm from the same department."

The preacher visited a home where the daughter had gone very far astray and the mother was trying to explain the circumstances. The preached asked, "Would you describe your daughter as being 'lewd'?" She answered, "No not yet, but she sure will be if she keeps running around."

Our local veterinarian told us about a man who brought his dog in to get its tail bobbed. The vet told him it would ruin the dog's looks if he had his tail cut off. The man insisted, "I want it off! My mother-in-law is coming to visit and I don't want her to see any sign that she is welcome!'

A preacher was eating chicken in a local restaurant. He said to the waiter, "This chicken must have been raised in an incubator." "So it was", the waiter replied, "but how did you know?" The preacher answered, "Well any chicken that was raised by a mother couldn't be as tough as this!"

Three preachers had enjoyed a chicken dinner at a farmer's home. After the meal the farmer took them out to see the barn. The rooster with his head held high crowed with loud vigor. One of the ministers said, "That is a very cocky rooster." The farmer replied, "You'd be cocky too if you had three sons who just entered the ministry."

A young bride went to do her first grocery shopping. She looked at the eggs and said to the grocer, "These are awfully small eggs." The grocer, replied, "I know, but it's the kind the famer brings me." "Well" she said, "That's the trouble with some farmers. They are so anxious to get their eggs sold, they take them off the nest too early!"

Wife: "Did you see the fur coat Mrs. Myers had on at church today?"
Husband: "No I didn't."
Wife: "Well did you see that hat Mrs. Brown had on?"
Husband: "No I didn't."
Wife: "Well all I can say is that it doesn't do you much good to go to church!"

A preacher was busy digging his car our of a mud hole where it had become stuck. A nosy passerby stopped and asked, "Is your car stuck in the mud?" The preacher replied, "No. The car died on me and I'm digging a hole to bury it in."

A preacher said to the mechanic, "I hope you won't charge me too much for fixing my car. I'm just a poor preacher." The mechanic replied, "I know. I heard you last Sunday."

7 ANNOUNCEMENTS

"I will declare thy name unto my brethren: in the midst of the congregation will I praise thee." (Psalm 22.22)

Bulletins are interesting. I saw one at a visiting church that read, "In the morning service the Pastor speaks. On Sunday evening, 'What the Fool Said'."

In one church there was a group of women that met at night to provide service for the Lakeshore Mental Health facility. There was an article in the bulletin about their work and the headline read, "Night Women in Action". Men lined up to join them at the next meeting.

Another bulletin said, "The ladies of the church have cast off clothing of every kind and they may be seen in the basement of the church on Friday afternoon".

Another announced, "Those wishing to donate eggs for the children's Easter egg hunt will please lay them on the altar after the morning worship service".

A preacher was trying to get people to move up closer to the front during the announcements and he said, "Come on up here. I've never felt right in the hind end since I got saved."

The preacher lived next door to the church and he often rolled his pant legs up so he wouldn't get them wet as he walked across the grass to the church. One Sunday he forgot to roll them back down before the service. His wife noticed his pants legs so she wrote him a note and sent it up to the preacher. As the preacher was making the announcements, he unfolded the note and read aloud, "For Heaven's sake John, pull your pants down."

One preacher was announcing that a special offering was to be taken to defray the expenses of the new carpet. He said, "All those wishing to do something on the carpet, please come forward and get a piece of paper."

Music directors often announce, "Turn over in your hymn book."

Preachers will often say, "I'm going to read the names of the people that are sick in the bulletin."

The pastor announced, "This afternoon there will be a meeting in both the south and north ends of the church. Children will be baptized at both ends".

A note containing a prayer request was passed to the preacher to read. "George Bowmen, having gone to sea, his wife desires the prayers of the congregation for his safety." The preacher read, "George Bowmen, having gone to see his wife desires the prayers of the congregation for his safety."

A preacher had been really sick with a lung disorder. Finally he was able to get back to church and he wanted to thank the people for their kindness to him. He said, "I thank you dear friends for your prayers and concern for me. I am much better but still have a ways to go. If I felt as well above my belt as I do below, I would be fine."

8 PREACHING THE GOSPEL

"Go ye into all the world, and preach the gospel to every creature."
(Mark 16:15)

After the church service one lady said to the preacher, "You will never know what your sermons have meant to me. They've been like water to a drowning man!"

Another church member told the preacher, "You are such a great pastor! We didn't know a thing about sin before you came here."

A preacher was preaching about how shallow a lot of Christian lives seem to be. He said, "As I rode my horse through the woods to church this morning, I noticed a tree that had fallen across the path. I got out to move it and I noticed it was "doady" at the heart and hollow at the butt. Many of you are just like that and cannot stand!"

One preacher stood up to preach and he had forgotten to put on his suspenders and his pants dropped down. He said, "Every one of you close your eyes and bow your heads and we will pray." He was so upset by the time he got his pants up and the prayer over he said, "Friends I'm just stymied this morning!" He quickly dismissed the services and hurried home.

One Sunday a preacher was bringing a strong message and he got carried away and stomped his foot. The floor caved in and he dropped out of sight.

One preacher was speaking on the subject "Behold I come quickly" and he couldn't remember the rest of the verse and so he repeated it again, "Behold I come quickly" and again his memory failed him. He quoted it again and he leaned so far forward the pulpit stand went forward and he fell into the lap of a woman sitting on the front pew. He was very apologetic and she said, "That's all right young man. You told me three times you were coming and I should have moved out of the way."

Jack Johnson was a very forceful speaker. One Sunday he brought a rock to the pulpit. During the sermon he said, "I'm going to throw this rock at the meanest man in town." He raised his hand up and six men hit their heads on the pews in front of them trying to get out of the way.

The preacher was preaching on the scripture from 2 Timothy that says, "But evil men and seducers shall wax worse and worse, deceiving and being deceived". In his haste, he said, "The churches in our town are getting waxier and waxier."

One Sunday a young man came in after church had started and was looking around. The preacher said, "Young Man are you looking for salvation?" "No", the man replied, "I'm looking for Sal Jackson."

The preacher got real eloquent one Sunday while preaching on the wonder of God's creation. He said, "The God who made the mountains made the tiny grains of sand. The God who spread the clouds across the canopy of the sky made the rain drops. The God who made me made a daisy."

One Sunday the preacher had completed his sermon and had given the invitation and a woman came forward. The preacher asked, "How do you come?" meaning by profession of faith, by letter or by statement. She answered, "I came by bus today."

In Tennessee people liked to have testimony meetings. One night everyone had something they were thankful for but Uncle Jake. The preacher said, "Uncle Jake don't you have a good word to say about Jesus?" Uncle Jake slowly got to his feet because he was very crippled by arthritis and he said, "Well I'll tell you preacher, he might nigh ruint me."

Brother Isabel was giving his testimony one Sunday. While recounting how he got started out in his career, a slip of the lips caused him to say, "I am thankful so many people helped me get started on my rear."

One hot July day a man that did shift work and had worked all night was in church on Sunday morning. My husband was talking about how careful we should be in our actions so as not to discourage others from becoming Christians. He said, "Sometimes it's like we shut the doors of our churches by the way we act." The man woke up to hear "shut the doors of our church". He walked all the way to the back of the sanctuary, shut the doors and walked back to his seat before he realized what he had done.

One preacher began his sermon by explaining, "When I shaved this morning I had my mind on my sermon and I cut my chin." After church one of the deacons said to the preacher, "Preacher, you would have done better to have had your mind on your chin and cut your sermon."

As a preacher finished his sermon, he looked down and noticed he still had on his bedroom slippers. He said to the congregation, "I will not go to the door this morning. I want you to leave speaking to no one as you continue to meditate on the sermon."

A guest preacher was getting ready to speak when he discovered his dental plate was broken and without his teeth, he couldn't speak. He whispered to the Master of Ceremonies that he would have to cancel his speech and explained the circumstances. "Oh I can fix that", said the MC, "I have an extra upper plate in my pocket." The preacher put the plate in but it didn't fit. He told the MC "No, I still can't speak". The MC brought out a second plate and finally a third which fit perfectly. After his speech, the preacher thanked the MC and said, "I sure am glad you're a dentist. You saved me today!" The MC replied, "I'm not a dentist, I'm an undertaker."

There was a country preacher and his wife who had seven children and they were so poor they always dressed in well-worn hand me downs. One Sunday the wife and children were running late. The preacher went ahead with the scripture reading from Matthew 6, "Consider the lilies of the field, how they grow; they toil not neither do they spin: And yet I say unto you, 'That even Solomon is all his glory was not arrayed like one of these'." In walked his wife and kids.

A man had been going from church to church trying to find the right one. Finally he went to one and the congregation was reading, "We have left undone those things which we ought to have done, and we have done those things we ought not have done." He joined the church that day and told the preacher, "I've found my crowd at last!"

A preacher was trying to express his desire to be available to help members of the congregation at any time. He said, "I am anxious to help you in any way I can as long as it's dishonorable."

One church never paid the traveling preacher. They would always say, "You will get your reward in the resurrection." Finally the preacher responded, "Yes brother, I know, but my old horse won't have a resurrection and he'd appreciate something to eat today."

My husband's father pastored small country churches and one night not many were there for the service. He passed his hat around to collect the offering and when it came back it didn't have any money in it. He said, "Well let's have a prayer and thank the Lord that I got my hat back."

9 SPECIAL OCCASIONS

"For where two or three are gathered together in my name, there am I in the midst of them." (Matthew 18:20)

Weddings were always a hoot. William Green was being married to Lucille Leg. The preacher in his confusion asked, "William, do you take this woman that you hold by the leg to be your lawful wife?"

At one wedding my husband dropped the ring. It bounced back up and he caught it and went right on with the ceremony as if nothing happened.

At a wedding the preacher often says at the end, "Now it's customary to kiss the bride". In the preacher's confusion, he said, "It is now "kissamary" to cuss the bride."

Mr. Phillip Thorn was being married and the preacher prayed, "Lord, bless this young couple and help them so there will not be too many thorns in their pathway."

An older man and woman came to the parsonage to get married. My husband asked them if they were about ready to stand up for the ceremony. The man called me aside and said, "Can you tell me where I can get her a bosom flower?" I went to the yard and got her a rose.

A girl getting married said to her mother, "I hate to leave you and Dad." Her mother replied, "Oh, that's oaky. You can take him with you!"

Another couple came to our house in LaFollette asking to be married. Their license was issued in Kentucky so Ervin told them he couldn't marry them in Tennessee. They really wanted him to marry him that day, so he drove them over the state line and married them in the backseat of the car.

One man and woman came to get married and at the close the man said to the preacher, "What do I owe you?" The preacher replied, "Whatever you think she is worth." The man said, "Well preacher I will be forever in your debt" and left without paying a penny.

Baptisms can sometimes cause a chuckle. One eighty-year-old man was to be baptized and the baptistery was one that was under the pulpit stand. When you were baptized you had to move the pulpit and open a hole to the baptistery by raising a trap door. The candidate to be baptized had to enter the sanctuary and walk into the water before the congregation. The man came forward, stuck his foot in the water and said, "Oh gosh Preacher, that cold water would kill a man my age!" He turned and walked right back out.

A boy "didn't have all that was coming to him" but he loved the Lord and wanted to be baptized. The baptism was held at the river and several had come out of the water saying, "Praise the Lord" or "Thank you Jesus". The boy came out of the water and yelled, "Hi-Yo Silver!" and went swimming on down the river.

Rev. Longshore was a preacher at Roadhiss, North Carolina years ago. He was baptizing a woman in the river and her wig came off in his hand. He handed it to the deacon who was helping him and the deacon threw it up on the river bank like it was alive. Rev. Longshore said afterward that if her head had come off he wouldn't have been more shocked. He swore he would never baptize a woman again unless he asked her first if she had on a wig.

The preacher baptized a woman and she had made her dress out of feed sacks. When it got wet, "Ballard's Best" came out across the back side. I heard a man ask, "Was it self-rising?"

A Presbyterian preacher came to my husband and asked if he could use our baptistery. He explained that the man wanted to be immersed and wanted a private service with only family in attendance. Ervin showed him the robe he wore and the boots and how to enter the baptistery and went back into his study. In a little while he heard this terrible yelling, "Help! Help! Help!" The preacher had put the rubber boots on the man to be baptized versus himself, and when he immersed the man they filled with water. It took quite some doing to get him out!

The preacher's son was six years old when he made his profession of faith and was baptized. The next morning he came to breakfast and he said good morning to his mom and kissed her as usual but he didn't speak to his father. His mother said, "Aren't you going to speak to you father." Their son replied, "No! He came within an inch of drowning me last night!"

My husband was preparing for the Lord's Supper one Sunday morning. A large fly kept buzzing around and he finally acknowledged it by saying, "It looks like we have a guardian angel this morning." About that time it dropped right out of the sky and into the communion plate!

In Chattanooga, Tennessee, Mr. Patton owned the large Patton Hotel. He put a one-dollar bill in the offering plate every Sunday and his secretary would send in his weekly offering on Monday. One Sunday we were having the Lord's Supper and Mr. Patton put his dollar bill on top of the communion bread as the plate was passed.

Funerals can sometime bring unexpected results. At one funeral, the husband of the woman who had died had the gravestone already engraved. The preacher was shocked when he read the inscription, "She was a good woman but now her end is up."

A farmer's mule kicked his mother-in-law and she died from her injury. A large crowd gathered for the funeral and most were men. The minister said, "Mrs. Baily must have been very popular. Just look at how many people are here." The farmer replied, "They ain't here for the funeral. They're here to bid on the mule."

ABOUT THE AUTHOR

Anneal Triplett Ledbetter was born on October 20, 1917 in Lenoir, North Carolina to Grover Bernhardt Triplett and Alma Moretz Triplett . Her unusual first name was a combination of the names of two of her aunts. According to family lore, Alma hoped to gain the good graces of her sisters-in-law by naming her daughter for both of them. Unfortunately neither was very happy with the combined result!

Anneal, Alma & Grover Triplett (1917)

Anneal came from a long line of strong women. Her paternal grandmother Julia Cornelia Triplet ran a boarding house in Lenoir. Her mother Alma received her teaching certificate from Appalachian Training School in Boone, North Carolina. She often rode on horseback to Lenoir to teach and stayed at the boarding house where she met her husband Grover. Following her marriage and the birth of her children, she decided to open a business and established Triplett

Clothing Company. She kept the books for the store and her husband's dairy farm for many years.

Anneal's father Grover graduated from Catawba College where he studied to become a watch maker. He spent much of his early career as an architect and builder. He and his partner E. A. Poe established the Poe Triplett Construction Company and were responsible for some of the older buildings on the campus at Appalachian State Teachers College in Boone and The Mayview Manor Hotel in Blowing Rock. Following a fire at Bernhardt's Furniture, he was responsible for the rebuilding. When it was finished he was asked to stay on and became their plant manager. After his retirement, he bought an interest in Blowing Rock Furniture Company. His hobby was dairy farming and he established and owned Triplett's Dairy which specialized in Guernsey milk. In 1923 Grover designed and built their family home in Lenoir, North Carolina, based on the stucco homes that he admired while working in Savannah, Georgia. Most of the original furniture in the home was created by Grover's brother-in-law and master carver, T. J. Stone.

Hand-Carved Furniture by T. J. Stone

Anneal had one younger brother, Ralph Grover Triplett who was born July 29, 1925. He met his wife June M. Guinn at Baylor University in Waco, Texas. Ralph was a successful business man and entrepreneur in Lenoir, North Carolina.

He and June had five children, Michael Ralph, Linda Jean, Patricia Neal, Timm Guinn and Shawn Todd. The Triplett and Ledbetter families shared numerous holidays, vacations and simple, happy times together.

Ralph Grover Triplett (1949)

After graduation from Mars Hill High School, Mars Hill, North Carolina, Anneal attended college at Queens University in Charlotte, where she was a member of Alpha Delta Pi sorority, Senior Representative of the Student Christian Association and President of the League of Evangelical Studies. She graduated with a degree in Home Economics. She earned her Master's Degree in Religious Education from Southern Baptist Theological Seminary in Louisville, Kentucky in 1939 where she met her husband James Ervin Ledbetter. Ervin was a graduate of Carson-Newman College in Jefferson City, Tennessee prior to earning his Master's Degree in Religious Studies at Southern Seminary.

Anneal Triplett & Ervin Ledbetter (1940)

Anneal and Ervin were married on September 12, 1940, at her home church in Lenoir, North Carolina, and served together for over fifty-two years prior to his death on August 28, 1992. During their marriage they ministered to congregations throughout East Tennessee including churches in Bristol, Elizabethton, Crossville, Lenoir City and LaFollette. Anneal also taught school and kindergarten at times throughout their marriage. After Ervin's retirement they continued to serve in interim ministries in Caldwell County, North Carolina.

Anneal and Ervin adopted two children, James Ervin, Jr. in 1948 and Miriam Hannah in 1949. Both children were loved unconditionally and were brought up in a caring, supportive, Christian home.

Anneal, Hannah, James & Ervin (1949)

Anneal was a devoted mother, grandmother and great-grandmother. Spending time with her family was one of her greatest joys.

Great-Granddaughters Katie & Claire Hopson, Son James Ledbetter, Grandson Matt Powell, Daughter Hannah Powell, Granddaughter Janet Nummi with Anneal Ledbetter on her 98th Birthday (2015)

Anneal loved to sew, knit, crochet and read until she began to suffer from macular degeneration. She never let that slow her down however, and she continued teaching Sunday School, leading Bible studies, serving as a deacon in her church and speaking throughout the community. She taught English as a second language for many years and volunteered at the local elementary school. She received the prestigious L.A. Dysart Citizenship Award for her service to the community.

The Anneal Ledbetter Sunday school class at First Baptist Church, Lenoir, North Carolina, was a second family to Anneal following Ervin's death and their love and support meant so much to her. When she made the decision to remain in Lenoir, she knew she would be some distance from her children, but could not leave her church family. When she passed away many of them were surrounding her bedside, singing hymns and praying. It was just as she would have wanted it to be.

Anneal collected angels throughout her life and had over a hundred in her collection most of which were gifts from friends and family.

Anneal Ledbetter and Angel Collection (2010)

Following Anneal's death on December 8, 2015, her family home was given to the Education Foundation of Caldwell County and was named the Angel

Center to commemorate her cherished collection of angel figures. The Executive Director of the foundation and force behind the reconstruction was Anneal's niece, Pat Triplett. When interviewed about the opening of the center, Pat remarked, "She not only collected angels, but she also was one."

Anneal & Ervin Ledbetter Angel Center (2019)

ACKNOWLEDGEMENTS

Many thanks to all of the family members and friends that helped bring this book to fruition. It was always our mother's dream to see her stories published and it's been a true labor of love to finally make it happen.

Mother's talented first grandchild, Janet Ledbetter Nummi (Art Director & Production Manager of www.JanetNummi.com) provided the cover design as well as photographic restoration and editing.

Her beloved cousin and artist, Evelyn Guire Allen of Lenoir, North Carolina, painted the beautiful watercolor on the front cover.

Watercolor artist, Judy Greene Prevost, provided the back cover portrait that captures Mother's joyful spirit. She also painted a lovely portrait that hangs in Mother's Sunday School classroom at First Baptist Church in Lenoir, North Carolina.

Our dear friend retired Army Lieutenant Colonel Sharie Hausser Russell, provided a much-needed set of fresh eyes for proof-reading and editing. Sharie is a "sister of the heart" and she and Mother shared many laughs together over the years.

A special thanks to our cousin, Pat Triplett, Executive Director of the Education Foundation Inc. of Caldwell County, a non-profit organization that supports high academic achievement and innovation in Caldwell County's public schools. Pat's efforts in fund-raising and overseeing the restoration of the Angel House have provided much-needed resources for the community and saved the historic house our grandfather built for future generations.

Thank-you to Dr. Frank L. (Pete) Charton and his wife Sylvia, our long-time friend and neighbor, for their encouragement and advice on self-publishing.

Many thanks to Gary and Peggy Shore for their invaluable friendship, love, assistance and counsel in coordinating Mother's physical and medical needs with us. It eased our minds immeasurably knowing that they were looking out for Mother in our absence.

The leadership and congregation of the First Baptist Church of Lenoir, North Carolina, meant so much to Mother over the course of her life. Additionally, each and every church our parents served throughout their years of ministry provided many blessed memories several of which are captured in this collection.

Finally, a heartfelt thank you to all of the members of the Anneal Ledbetter Sunday School class. They were such a wonderful support system to her throughout her time in Lenoir and have been so encouraging in seeing her book published. There are so many individual members that have provided prayers, love, companionship, fellowship, transportation, home repairs, medical advice, audio tapes, and so much more. She especially loved all the holiday celebrations and her own special Santa Claus (Ron Stillwell). Each and every class member had a very special place in her heart.

James Ledbetter and Hannah Powell

Made in the USA
Coppell, TX
05 July 2020

30208038R00028